A NEW CHRIST
BY

Wallace D. Wattles

FOREWORD

Wallace D. Wattles (1860-1911) was an American author who wrote books on the New Though and self-help movements. Wattles best known book is *The Science of Getting Rich*. This version of *The Science of Getting Rich* includes a table of contents.

A New Christ

INTRODUCTION The Great Adventure Ahead

HERE we cannot stay. Our very existence demands that we go forward or backward. Life is not static. Change and movement are in the picture for all of us. Whether for better or for worse, move we must. Today we are moving into that next great forward step from self-consciousness into cosmic- or God-consciousness. We are beginning to understand that we must lose ourselves, lose our egocentric occupation, throw wide the bars, give our lives away, and get into a higher consciousness where we know that none of us can live without the others, none can be completely happy and safe unless all are happy and safe.

In our world, man has had freedom of choice from the earliest time. He chose his path in the beginning, and if his first choice was stupid, there were new opportunities coming along for him to better his condition. Good or bad, wise or unwise, he has made his choices. If some super-auditor could produce a tally sheet of man's decisions over the ages, we wonder how the two columns would compare. Which influence has been the stronger, constructive or destructive, good or bad? We wonder where our freedom has been leading us, for now we come up against what seems to be the grave issue of survival in the atomic age.

Today the choice before us is a definite and a vital one. We see it and recognize it. It is not lurking in the shadows, like a thief in the night waiting to surprise us; it is not out of sight over the horizon like a distant tornado which we need not fear. No, the issue today is clear and ominous. If we use atomic fission in the world of force, we face doom. We are compelled this time really to look at the two ways which Jesus told us about, the way of Caesar which is the way of violence and force, and the way of the Kingdom of God, which is the way of co-operation, compassion and fellowship. If we think thoughts of Caesar's world we give our allegiance to Caesar; but if we think the thoughts of Jesus, our allegiance is to the Highest Power for good.

We have our dream, every man's dream for a more abundant life. And we dare not make a stupid choice this time. Our decision will have farther-reaching consequences than anyone can estimate. Never in history has man been faced with anything comparable to it. Our great opportunity lies in choosing the way of compassion and love, the Kingdom of God way. Let us take hold of our dream for a more abundant life, fall on our knees with it, and commit ourselves to its fulfillment.

Man always has the choice. This is the free will that God gives him. And this free will is one of the most magnificent of God's gifts. One may ask, If God wants His children to be happy, healthy and peace- loving, why does He allow us to have feelings of depression, weakness, hatred and jealousy?

The answer is that we are not puppets. We are not little chessmen on a board, moved by some great power that is pushing us around. None of us likes to be pushed around. We can, for the most part, choose to do or be whatever we wish to. This is a magnificent freedom that God has given us. It puts tremendous power at our disposal. What wonderful results we see when we use it constructively! But we can use this power in reverse, and when we do so we pay. The satisfaction we anticipate turns to ashes in our mouth.

We would retain and respect the freedom that God has given us, even though we are aware that within it lies the possibility of both good and evil. We may be comforted by the knowledge that the freedom we may have spoiled by misuse can again be reversed by His love and be reborn in us the moment we give our lives and wills completely into His keeping. And so we seek the path of discipline not because we must, but because we want to. We want the best. We do it because it is wise; it is the way to the complete and abundant life we all desire. But the choice is voluntary.

Today religion is not so often saying "You must" and "You ought," since it is learning a better way to put it. Today religion is saying to us, "This is the way to find wholeness and happiness and fulfillment. The other way costs too much and it does not give you anything of value." This is the best use of free choice. It invites cooperation by making the better way seem reasonable, sensible and desirable. It makes possible a wholehearted decision to seek and follow the higher road. And it helps in achieving a singleness of purpose and an unchanging vision of a more perfect realm as our goal.

Our dream, through decision and preparation, can turn into a great and rewarding adventure. But how important is this singleness of purpose! Indifference, uncertainty, wavering between beliefs, between ideals, between goals, will weaken or nullify our hope of achievement. We cannot ride two horses when they are not going up the same road. Remember, there is no pretense in the soul. If we are to have the fullness of the power of prayer, if we are to know the heights of spiritual attainment, we must be absolutely true. We must live outwardly everything that we believe, and we must be careful that our lips do not say those things which we are not ready to live. We must be completely and wholly coordinated. That which we believe deep down within us will shout itself from the housetops. We deceive ourselves when we feel we can hide it. In the last analysis everything is known. When we are true to ourselves, "It follows as the night the day, that we can not then be false to any man."

The decision to embark upon this adventure to seek a more abundant life concerns ourselves first of all. So it is right that we should stop a moment and examine our motives. Why do we seek the abundant life? What do we mean by "abundant"? Obviously, the standard by which we weigh our answers to such questions is the standard of unselfishness. Are we self-seeking in our planning? "He that seeks to save his life shall lose it, and he that loses his life for my sake shall find it." said Jesus. So, in this glorious adventure we dare not be self-seeking. The world has long enough followed the road of cunning planning for selfish ends. Man has tried that sort of thing too long. W hat has it brought him?

Never before were these words of Jesus more true: "What shall it profit a man, if he shall gain the whole world, and lose his own soul?" Our mad scramble for material things, the desperate struggle for power supremacy among nations, our dependence upon intellectual rather than spiritual values, all have tended to push God farther and farther into the background. As a result, we have lost our sense of direction, and with storm clouds gathering, we know not whither to flee. At a moment like this, our worldly achievements are as nought compared with the peace we yearn for. We want to find our way again, and we want it not only for ourselves, but for the whole human race. Our soul's most sincere desire is that mankind everywhere will open its heart to be filled with compassion and love and goodwill toward men and toward God! Here, then, is our answer. This project is not for self-seekers. It is to be undertaken only by those visualizing a far more sublime achievement.

Our adventure will take us out over uncharted seas. It will put us on paths with which we have little or no acquaintance. There will be times when we shall wonder whether to go on or turn back. But God's promises are still good, and we shall not give up. It is His strength on which we shall be relying. Our faith will grow stronger as we acknowledge our own weakness and give over to Him the control, the management of every detail. If we let Him have His way, we shall find that we are being guided by the Holy Spirit into truths which will later, perhaps much later, become accepted as though men had always known them. These new, strange, fresh truths, full of dynamic power, might cause us, as mere human beings, to be afraid. But we shall be wearing the armor of God, our decision made, we shall fare forth with Him in faith.

St. Augustine said, "Faith is to believe what we do not see; and the reward of this faith is to see what we believe." We believe that faith is an attribute common to both science and religion. Outwardly the scientist's faith and the churchman's faith may not look alike at first glance. But there is much in common. The scientist and the religionist or mystic are both reaching out for something on which to pin their faith. In the lives and dreams of each of these men there are great areas uncharted and unexplored inviting them to adventure and discovery. In these great new areas both men know there is something deep, unchanging, unvarying. They both want to contact this Absolute, for there, they both know, they can pin their faith. There lies the answer to Man's problems. There, awaiting conquest by faith, rests the secret of fulfillment and perfection. These men may not both call this Absolute Power by the name of God, but it is God just the same. They both pin everything they have upon the knowledge of the laws of the universe as they see them. They both know these laws will not fail them.

We are studying the teachings of the world of physical science in connection with the study of spiritual values, for our unique purpose is to build a bridge between physical science and religious teaching. We want to see an agreement, a mutual tolerance, in that area where the intangible values cannot be measured by scale and test tube. And this is coming about even now. The physical scientists are supporting religion by their acknowledgment of powers beyond their explanation, and of the need of a higher reference than materialism in our complex life. And religion is accepting with a more open mind all of God's gifts, not fearing more knowledge but welcoming it as a part of His unfolding plan.

It is like two men who start off together, both of them intent upon climbing the unsealed Mountain of the Unknown. They soon disagree about the route. Each believes he knows the only way leading to the top, and so they part company. Years later they come face to face on a convergence of their paths. They greet each other in amazement, and compare notes on their journeys so far. They feel a new respect for each other. And then, realizing that they have gone only part of the way to the top, with the stiffer climb still ahead, they come to a new agreement. They will no longer ignore each other's beliefs, each other's leadings. They will keep in touch, and lend a helping hand when necessary.

In spite of grave danger today, the world is ready for a great forward step. That step can be taken if man can let go of the willful self sufficiently to be lifted up into that next evolutionary pattern that lies before him. Our faith, our lives, will then be geared to higher values, and the lesser things, the destructive things, will fall away.

Today as we work among people we see a new interest arising everywhere. There is a new reaching out. A yearning is in the hearts of men and women which they are not ashamed to express. There is a new seeking. And earnest seeking does not go unrewarded. New hope is showing in the faces of people, and there is a rekindling of faith that envisions a new world. Oh how the angels of heaven must be rejoicing as they see one, then ten, a hundred, a thousand, with their faith reborn and growing! This faith is the great bulwark of the sons of God, the rod and the staff to strengthen and comfort them in their need. It binds them close to God, yet blesses them with freedom and power for their challenging adventure.

There will be joy, enthusiasm and thrilling expectancy in the experiences ahead. There will also be trials, difficulties, disappointments, but not greater ones than we can bear. Our inner conditioning will determine the way we shall react to testing. Can we say with St. James, "Count it all joy, my brethren, when you meet various trials, for you know that the testing of your faith produces steadfastness"? If fears and doubts assail the citadel of our inner being, and we are tempted to let them enter, we shall call quickly upon our Divine Protector; for, as St. Paul has said, "God is faithful, and he will not let you be tempted beyond your strength.".

In this adventure of the spirit we shall not be wholly dependent upon our five senses, for in spiritual perception these wonderful physical gifts alone are inadequate. We shall know beyond our seeing, by virtue of faith. Peter put it this way: "Without having seen him you love him; though you do not now see him you believe in him and rejoice with unutterable and exalted joy. As the outcome of your faith you obtain the salvation of your souls."

We shall seek to develop constancy in our contact with the unseen spiritual forces. It will require patience, and prayer and love in great abundance. For we shall want to see through and beyond the three-dimensional world in order to attain more spiritual power, greater wholeness and a new capacity for achievement in the larger life.

We all have at least a spark of Divine fire within us. Each one of us has something of that high purpose, that urge to unselfish achievement, which we can lift to God for dedication. Let us take it, however small, and ask God to show us how best to use it. Though it be apparently insignificant as we hold it before Him, we need not be concerned. For He values greatly whatever we offer Him, if it be our best. He sees the great potential in our gift, and if we ask Him to tell us how to develop it, then listen carefully, He will direct us. He will lead us into the right action and we shall be justified in expecting great results.

We have no right to limit the mighty things God can do through us. We are His instruments and all we need to do is to let Him use us. Our part is to stop resisting–to get ourselves out of the way. As the little spark within us becomes a flame, as our tiny gift begins to develop, as we feel ourselves being used as channels of God's power, our spirits soar as on eagles' wings! This is a supreme moment. We become conscious of the Presence in our midst. We feel the Divine influx.

We feel our oneness with Him. He looks into us; nothing is hidden; He knows our every need. As we give ourselves completely to Him and lay our lives open to Him, ashamed of nothing, afraid of nothing, His understanding love encompasses us and our lives take on new meaning. A sense of glorious destiny fills us. We no longer feel inadequate, but we are consumed with a great desire to stride out ahead and beyond our earth-bound limitations.

We begin our search for the higher life. We start right where we are, looking at experiences and ideas from all sides, examining them and seeking more light on them. We revise many of our concepts, and re-evaluate much of our world.

As we continue, we find our goal to be a more expanded consciousness, a widened horizon of awareness. So through recognition and development of the idea of the interdependence of body, mind and spirit, we enlarge our philosophical circumference. From the very start, in this quest, we instinctively reach out for a Higher Intelligence. We become aware of that Divine Something within us which we do not fully comprehend, but which we know somehow is the key to man's unfoldment. At last we see that it is the Christ-self within us which relates us to God's love, and brings into our life the limitless power of the universe.

We see the importance of this not only for ourselves but for others. We feel an awakening sense of mission. How can we spread the good news? How can we best be a channel for bringing the light and love of God and the awareness of the Christ-self to others? We begin to realize that it is through the development of the Christ-self in ourselves.

Working in these areas we find ourselves growing in understanding, walking on higher paths, gaining in both spiritual insight and outlook. We reach a new plateau of enlightened vision, and from here we can see ahead an ever-expanding vista of beauty and perfection. We are awed and shaken by its magnitude. It is unfathomable, mysterious, yet full of such radiant promise as we have never known. The adventure of life so far has unfolded many wonders. But in the greater adventure beyond, we will find mature spiritual achievement, and fulfillment of our destiny.

Proceeding along the way we have just envisioned, we pray for deep in filling. We welcome every experience that comes to us in our day- to-day development. We find in ourselves an ever-increasing devotion to our high purpose, and an ever-deepening joy in our mission. Setbacks become less frequent, and when they do occur we are not discouraged by them. We but count them as stepping-stones out of darkness into light. Edison counted his failures as just so many methods proven unworkable, and so do we.

Confidence in our higher self grows in proportion to our relationship with Christ. It is when we have a knowledge of belonging that we feel an inner reinforcement. Courage and self-assurance are ours in increased measure when we identify with greatness beyond our own. W ho are we, then? From whence cometh our courage and our strength? Jesus made the startling statement, "You have not chosen me, it is I who have chosen you". What amazing love is expressed here! We are His! By His own words we are chosen to carry His love in our hearts and to give it out to all. "By this shall all men know that ye are my disciples, if ye have love one to another." This love is our identification with Him. As we give it out we are, as Paul said, "ambassadors for Christ, God making his appeal through us", for the whole world.

When the Master walked this earth, love among men did not extend far beyond family boundaries. The tight little circle of family and race had to be enlarged to include all men, all nations, for His was a radical teaching for His day. Even now there are those who quarrel with such an all-inclusive concept. Yet it was the crowning idea of His ministry, and He lived it and died for it because He knew that love in the hearts of men was the only hope for the world's salvation. We must learn to love people with the same intensity, the same compassion as we have for our very own. We must love in them their potential good, and pray for that quality to express itself.

Jesus realized as He taught the disciples, that He was stretching their provincialism, and expanding their love circumference. He wanted them to reach out with this kind of caring to those beyond their family and their nationalism. That is why He posed the questions, "W ho is my brother? W ho is my sister? W ho is my mother?" He was creating in them the expanded consciousness of their relationship with all men, of love for all people. And this is what we must learn today.

Specifically, we must learn to love our neighbor. But loving our neighbor sometimes puts us to quite a test. The less we feel naturally drawn to certain people, the more difficult it seems for us to love them. The trouble is that we transfer our dislikes from the deeds of a man to the man himself. Love does not flow. It is dammed up by the way in which we ourselves react. So we correct the matter by learning to love the man instead of what he does. Then love is released and our identity with God is strengthened.

We learn to love a person as a child of God, recognizing in them a potential quality much greater than their deeds may demonstrate. In this we are not overlooking their mistakes, but extending to them a compassionate understanding through our love and prayers. But if we find one who insists upon going their selfish, willful way, then we have but one thing to do–stand by and wait, just as the Master waits for us. We never stop loving and praying for them, yet we do not hurry them. Until they are ready we can do nothing more than this. Then suddenly a miracle may happen. But whether it happens or not is really not our responsibility if we have fulfilled our part of loving and praying. In this we strengthen our identity with the Father, and as that is made stronger, our spiritual influence with others is increased.

We mentioned earlier the need for man to let go of the willful self to enable him to be lifted up into his next evolutionary spiritual pattern. We must surrender the selfish, grasping, ruthless part of man's nature, that part of him which promotes himself at the expense of others, is quick to blame others, harbors resentments and worries, and is indeed altogether unlovely. We do not mean the strong, individualized characteristics which make men outstanding in constructive, human achievement. In the giving up of the little self we need not be at all worried that we shall be giving up our individuality. W hen we are reborn into the higher self we shall have far more individuality. We shall find ourselves more unique. We shall develop along our own distinctive lines and as a result we shall be different from one another.

We may well look at the disciples and see how they developed. As they grew in grace they did not grow more alike in characteristics. They became alike only in their consecration and zeal, in their lifted consciousness. But in their several personalities, their outward expression, they were as different as snowflakes, no two of which are ever alike. We may expect this kind of development, each toward his or her own perfection, without any of the things that cause trouble and disturbance within us, and through that disturbance, disease of the body.

It is the willful self that tries to oppose the current of life by making its own plan, setting its own pattern and insisting on that being fulfilled. This stubborn opposition to God's laws of life often brings a sharp crisis in man's affairs, and he cries out, "O God, why did you do this to me?" But even in the crisis, Christ is present, and man would see Him there, if his lack of humility did not blind him. Humility–true humility–not only brings us to the place where God's help can enter our lives, it insures us of His repeated help, and we cannot ask too often. A habit of humble asking enables us to contact Him at any time instantly.

Saul of Tarsus was reduced to utter humility and while in that state he found the Great Power which lifted him into a higher expression and he was no longer Saul. He became Paul. Just as Peter had been changed from Simon the unstable to Peter the Rock. But, time after time, both of these men slipped, lost their footing for just a fraction of time and went down. But they never stayed down. All they had to do was to lie still for just long enough to contact the Power again, and they got up and went on. They were enabled to do this because in their humility they were no longer encumbered by the petty, egocentric self. Their lives had been turned outward from the center and they could again function in the dimension of Divine creativity.

We glimpse the constructive, limitless possibilities of the higher life and everything we do is turned toward its realization. We are aware of negative emotions that must be transformed into constructive forces. For instance, suppose we are perfectionists–suppose we are drivers with a tremendous inner urge that doesn't let us rest. The "hound of heaven" pounding close behind always pursues us. If we do not find a constructive expression for this type of nature, we are going to use it negatively. We grow fussy and domineering. We are likely to become a gorgeous nuisance! People may admire us but they won't like us. Because we are not using our drive, our perfectionism, for big things. We must redirect the wasted energy of irritability, fault-finding and criticism, and make it work for something constructive and worthwhile.

Man has harnessed the forces of nature everywhere to relieve himself of labor and give himself time for many other things. The next step, our next duty, is to harness and control and use the emotional drive to create a new world, a world where jealousy, hatred and fear are replaced by love.

Motivated by a vision of building a new world, we have no time for indulging in negative thoughts and emotions. With our energies focused upon bringing the Kingdom of Heaven to earth, we do not feel repressions. The sophisticated world may wag its finger at us and warn us that we will have to deny ourselves lots of good things. But the world is wrong. We are not living a deprived life. We are not denied any good thing. We are not living the life of withdrawal, the one-sided narrow existence, restricted by intolerance, fear and superstition. No, instead it is a life of fulfillment. We enjoy a trinity of blessings, spiritual, mental and physical. There is an old saying, "Make your passion write poetry." This means that everything in life can be lifted up to a higher expression; for it all comes from God, and His gifts are free and without blemish. Only man limits, binds down, misuses, mars and destroys.

When we make full use of God's gifts, we shall find fulfillment. We shall find the perfect things we are to express. He will create in us through His indwelling Spirit, and bring into visible form, original ideas, inventions, art, music, poetry, that will delight His children.

* * * * *

In the chapters that follow you are going to meet, perhaps for the first time, the real Jesus of Nazareth. You will learn what kind of man He really was, and what His true mission and purpose on earth was.

Wallace Wattles is best known for his book "The Science of Getting Rich", published in 1910, in which he provides a formulated system for acquiring wealth by harnessing and utilizing the power of creative thought. He went on to write several other books along similar lines including "The Science of Being Well", "The New Science of Living and Healing", and The Science of Being Great."

"A New Christ" was Wattles' very first book and has been virtually forgotten about having been out of print for the past hundred years, yet it remains one of the finest, if not the finest book on primitive Christianity ever written. In it he describes with brilliant clarity what Jesus the man really stood for, and why He was despised and put to death. He goes on to explain what Jesus meant when He said "The works that I do, you shall do also, and much greater works", and how this can really be so.

Part two of the book, "Jesus: The Man and His Works", was originally privately published as a book based on a lecture that Wattles gave in Cincinnati, Ohio in 1905. His lecture made such a favorable impression on some of his listeners that they determined to have it printed if Professor Wattles would provide a manuscript. As the lecture was based on his book "A New Christ", quite a lot of his original book is duplicated in "Jesus: The M an and His Works", however it is still well worth reading as there are a number of very interesting and amusing anecdotes included, and also some further insights that were not included in his first book.

Part three of the book centers around a famous inspirational lecture entitled "The Greatest Thing in the World" that the Scottish evangelist Henry Drummond gave at a mission station in Central Africa in 1883. The American evangelist Dwight L. Moody heard Drummond's talk the following year and said he had never heard anything so beautiful. Based on the Bible's "love chapter," 1 Corinthians 13, the lecture was made into a pamphlet and has since become a classic with over 12 million copies out over the 120 years it has been in print.

A second lecture by Drummond entitled "The Programme of Christianity," is included, and you will find that it blends perfectly with the first two sections of this book by Wallace Wattles. It is quite likely that Wattles would have had opportunity to read these lectures by Drummond before writing his own book, and it may well have been those that originally inspired him. Certainly Drummond has been quoted extensively in other's writings ever since his lectures were published.

Although both Drummond and Wattles came from Christian backgrounds, and were both ordained ministers, their teachings transcend organized religion completely, so no matter what your own particular religion may be, or if you have no religion at all, you are sure to find great value in reading what they have to say.

Chapter 1 - His Personality

This series will not be an attempt to prove something about Christ; it will be an effort to ascertain by scientific study, what He was, how He lived, and what He taught. Too many people have studied Jesus from the standpoint of some preconceived notion of Him or His mission, such an attitude always leads to erroneous conclusions.

The common concept of Christ was given to the church by the priests of the dark ages, at a time when a religious ideal was wanted which should induce men to be content with slavery, and to bow their necks to every kind of wrong and oppression; and this concept was drawn almost wholly from the poetry of Isaiah; the Christ of the churches is the Christ of Isaiah, and our ideas of Him are not drawn at all from an impartial study of the history of His life.

Such passages in the prophecies as; "He is despised and rejected of men; a man of sorrows and acquainted with grief; and we hid, as it were, our faces from him; he is brought as a lamb to the slaughter, and as a sheep before her shearers is dumb, so he opened not his mouth," have been quoted to show His character, and the meekness and humbly submissive spirit with which He endured wrong and injustice; and we have had held up as the ideal man a despised, friendless, poverty-stricken laborer whom the upper classes regarded with scorn because of his lowly origin and station; who had no friends save fishermen, laborers, outcasts and sinners; who was often shirtless and hungry, and who bore insults and persecutions with meek submission, and walked about in a scornful world with his hands always uplifted in loving benediction.

This character has too long been offered as the Christian ideal; Be meek, Be submissive, Be lamb-like or sheep-like. Bow your head before the persecutor, and offer your back to the shearer. Rejoice when you are fleeced; it is for the glory of God. It is a good religion for the man with the shears.

The Christ who was held up in the old fashioned orthodox pulpit is a weak character. He is not the kind of a man we would nominate for president, and his followers have very little faith in him as an organizer.

No railroad magnate of today would make him foreman of a section; and if it were broadcast over the country tonight that the president of the United States had resigned and that Jesus would be inaugurated tomorrow, 95 percent of the Christians there would draw their money out of the banks for fear Jesus might start a panic.

What we propose to do now is to ascertain by a study of the four gospels in the light of history whether this is the real Christ; and if not, to find what the real Christ was like.

The Real Jesus Christ . In the first place, then, Jesus could not have been despised because He was a carpenter, or the reputed son of a carpenter. Custom required every Jewish Rabbi or teacher to have a trade. We read in the Talmud of Rabbi Johanan, the blacksmith, and of Rabbi Isaac, the shoemaker, learned and highly honored men. Rabbi Jesus, the carpenter, would be spoken of in the same way. St. Paul, a very learned man, was a tent-maker by trade.

At that time, and among that people, Jesus could not have been despised for His birth and station.

And He was popularly supposed to be of royal blood, being saluted as the son of David; His lineage was well known. The people who cried "Hosannah to the son of David" knew that He was an aristocrat of the aristocrats; a prince of the royal house. He was not "lowly" in birth, nor was He supposed to be so. On this point I refer you to Matthew 9:27; Matthew 15:22; Matthew 20:30; Matthew 21:9; M ark 10:47.

He W as Educated . Second, He could not have been despised for His ignorance, for He was a very learned man. Whenever He went into a synagogue He

was selected to read the law and teach the congregation, as the one best qualified for that work. Luke says; "There went a fame of Him through all the region round about, and He taught in their synagogues, being glorified of all." In those times of fierce religious disputation, no unlearned man could have held his own in such fashion. He must have been letter-perfect in the books of the Jewish law, for He was always able to rout His adversaries by making apt quotations from their own books. Even His enemies always addressed Him as Master, or Teacher, acknowledging His profound learning. On this point, read Matthew 13:54; Mark 12:24-34; Luke 4:14-15; John 7:19-23; John 10:34.

Jesus Had Plenty . Third, He was not despised for His poverty, for He had many wealthy and influential friends, and knew no lack of anything. Lazarus and his sisters, whose home was always open to Him, were people of consequence; for we are told that "many of the Jews" came to comfort the sisters when Lazarus died.

Luke says that Joanna, the wife of Chuza, the king's steward, and other women "ministered unto him of their substance"; that is, they were supporters of His work.

The king's steward was a high official, and his wife would be a prominent lady.

Joseph of Arimathea, who came to get the body of Jesus, was a well- to-do man. So, probably was Nicodemus.

Jesus healed the sick in the families of rulers and high officials, and they appear to have responded liberally in supplying His financial needs.

True, He held no property and bought no real estate; but He dressed expensively, lived well and never lacked for money. W hen He was crucified the soldiers cast lots for His clothing because it was too fine to cut up, as they would have done with the garments of an ordinary man; and on the night of His betrayal, when Judas went

out, it was supposed by the others that he had gone to give something to the poor. It must have been their custom to give away money, or how could such a supposition have arisen? In that country and climate, the wants of Jesus and His disciples were few and simple, and they seem to have been fully supplied. He wore fine clothes, had plenty to eat and drink, and had money to give away. Read Luke 8:1-3; Luke 5:33; Luke 23:50; John 11:19; John 12:2; John 19:23.

Jesus W as Not Humble . Fourth, Jesus was not humble, in the commonly accepted meaning of the word. He was a man of the most impressive, commanding and powerful personal appearance. He "spoke as one having authority" and "his word was with power."

Frequently, we are told, great fear and awe fell upon the people at His mighty words and works. In one place they were so frightened that they besought Him to leave; and John tells how certain officers sent to arrest Him in the market place lost their nerve in His commanding presence, and went back, saying "Surely, never man spake like this man."

On the night of His arrest a band of soldiers approached Him in the grove and asked for Jesus of Nazareth; and when He answered "I am he," such was His majesty and psychic power that they prostrated themselves; "they went backward," the account says, "and fell to the ground" (John 18:6).

To be like the Christ of the four Gospels, one must be learned, well dressed, well supplied with money, and of noble and commanding appearance, speaking with authority, and having tremendous magnetic power. And now, what was His attitude toward His fellow men?

Chapter 2 - His Attitude

One of the very best ways to reach an understanding of Jesus is by studying His reasons for taking the title He assumed - the Son of Man. He rarely spoke of Himself in any other way. This term, Son of Man, was common in the Jewish prophecies, and in the current conversation of the times, and it was simply an emphatic way of saying "Man." If you wished to emphasize your fealty to democracy, you might say "I am a son of Thomas Jefferson"; and if you wished to emphasize your fealty to humanity, you would say as Jesus did. "I am a son of man."

The World Jesus Lived In . The Roman empire was a great taxing machine. In its conquered provinces, the people were left, as far as possible, with their own local government and institutions of justice, the function of the Roman officials being to extort tribute, or collect taxes. Every form of extortion and oppression was practiced by the governors, procurators and tax collectors upon those who had property. Open robbery, torture, kidnapping, false accusation and imprisonment might be visited upon the man who had money to tempt the cupidity of the higher powers; and as the oppressed property owners had no way of meeting the exactions of the government but by exploiting the poor, the condition of the masses was pitiful indeed.

You will readily see that the business, and property-owning class had to get the money to pay their taxes by exploiting the multitude in some way. It is an economic axiom which is indisputable that all taxation of whatever kind, upon whomsoever levied, must at last be wrung from the hard hands of the producers; no one, however, seems to comprehend this fact as little as the producers themselves. They strenuously reject all offers of deliverance, and generally kill those who try to help them.

Jesus received His only real and permanent following from among the middle class, as we shall see, and was crucified by the workers, whom He was trying to deliver from oppression. It was no middle class mob which demanded the liberation of Barabbas and howled for the blood of Christ.

To give you an idea as to how oppressive the Roman taxation was, we may estimate from certain passages in Josephus that the private income of Herod the Great was three and one-half millions of dollars a year. That is vastly less, of course, than the income of our John D. Rockefeller; but our Herods have a much larger, richer, and more populous country to levy taxes on, and they have discovered methods of extortion which lay the crude ways of the monarchs of antiquity very far in the shade. The enormous sums which were collected from the little province of Galilee brought the unhappy workers down to the last extremity of destitution; they could go no lower and live.

The Sects of Jesus' Day . In Judea at this time were several religious sects, which were also, in a way, political parties, scheming for prestige and power, and for influence with Rome. The Pharisees, Sadducees, Essenes, Samaritans, etc., disagreed upon various questions, as the existence or non-existence of angels, the resurrection of the dead, baptism, and so on. The strife between these parties was desperately acrimonious and bitter, often to the point of open violence. You will notice as you read that they were always ready to "take up stones" to end a dispute; riots were of daily occurrence in the streets of Jerusalem, and only the psychic power and commanding personality of Jesus saved Him from being stoned by these religious mobs. Read Luke 4:28-30; Luke 20:6; John 8:59.

The leaders of these sects were, of course, of the middle, or property-owning class; but the rank and file were the common masses, sunk in the most abject poverty - taxed, beaten, robbed, outraged, slaughtered, with no voice lifted anywhere in their behalf. No one, Jew or Gentile, thought for a moment of demanding justice for the mongrel multitude.

It is said of Jesus that He "had compassion on the multitude, because they fainted, and were amazed, and were like sheep without a shepherd" (Matthew 9:36). They had then, as now, plenty of

shepherds to baptize them, to interpret prophecy for them, to instruct them in "spiritual" things; but none to demand a lightening of their burdens - none to cry out, in their behalf, for justice.

The principal care of the shepherds was that the flock should be so doctrinally correct that they would never, never consent to be sheared by the opposing party.

The New Thought of Jesus' Time . Into this maze of oppression, taxation, murder, outrage and theological discussion comes the grand, strong figure of this young prince and scholar, saying; "The Spirit of the Lord is upon me, for he hath anointed me to preach good news to the poor. I am no Pharisee; I am no Sadducee, Essene, or Samaritan; I am a man. I come, not in behalf of Pharisaism or Samaritanism, but in behalf of humanity."

Here was an altogether different religious attitude; He had no "ism" to build up; His only creed was justice, His only doctrine the square deal. No wonder they were "amazed at his doctrine."

No wonder His "word was with power."

No wonder they said, "he speaketh as one having authority." Jesus said of Himself that the father had given Him authority to execute judgment because He was man (John 5:27). That is the only reason God could possibly have for giving authority to any man; if there is a man anywhere today upon whom the divine sanction rests, it is not because he is a Pharisee, a Methodist, Presbyterian, Republican or Democrat, but because he is a MAN.

And it is further true that amongst all those who claim leadership by virtue of divine authority we may apply this test with certainty - that the man who stands for humanity, first, last and all the time, against all vested interests, religious and economic, is the man who stands as Jesus stood.

The man who stands for humanity against the vested religious

interests of his time frequently is called an infidel; and the man who stands for the propertyless against the vested political and economic interests of his time is called a traitor. Jesus was crucified on the charges of infidelity and treason, and He was guilty on both counts.

Let no one be too horrified here to proceed further; for there are no prouder titles when justly held than the terms Infidel and Traitor. It was a grand saying of Wendell Phillips; "Write upon my grave. Infidel-Traitor; infidel to every church that compromises with wrong; traitor to every government that oppresses the poor."

The most sinful infidelity is not being unfaithful to some church, but being unfaithful to the truth; and the vilest treason is not turning against some government, but turning against the weak and helpless. This was the attitude which Jesus took; He gave expression to all this when He took the title which made Him the champion of humanity - when He said, "I am the Son of Man."

We will now take up the consideration of His teachings.

Chapter 3 - His Teachings About Man

If Jesus was a Savior, He came to save mankind, collectively and individually, from sin, from Error; for there is nothing but error to be saved from. That is what He says of Himself, in John 18:37; "To this end was I born, and for this cause came I into the world, that I should bear witness to the truth."

A lost world is a world which has lost the truth about life; and a lost man or woman is simply one who has lost the truth about life; and there is no other way under heaven to save the lost but by telling them the truth about life.

This simple sentence in which He concisely states His mission lets in a flood of light upon His theory of life; He came to save from sin, disease and poverty by telling the truth. Then sin, disease and poverty are untruths; that is, they are wrong ways of living. We will consider first His broader and more generic application of truth, and later, His application of it to the individual.

In the sermon on the mount, He says (Matthew 5:21-22); "Ye have heard that it was said by them of old time, thou shalt not kill; and whosoever shall kill shall be in danger of the judgment; but I say unto you, that whosoever is angry with his brother without a cause shall be in danger of the judgment; and whosoever shall say to his brother Raca, shall be in danger of the council; but whosoever shall say Thou fool, shall be in danger of hell fire." The phrase, "thou fool," as we understand it now, does not give the meaning of the original at all; it would be better rendered by some such phrase as "you are of no value" or "you are good for nothing."

I can make His meaning clear, I think, by an illustration. I was sitting in a hotel lobby, once, when the news came of a coalmine horror in which a number of poor fellows lost their lives. Two well- dressed men near me were discussing the affair, and one said; "Oh, well, it's only a couple of Huniaks less. A million more are ready to step into their shoes tomorrow; the world hasn't lost anything."

Jesus says whosoever shall speak of a man as that man spoke, is in danger of hell fire. That man, and those who think and speak as he does, are the real murderers of all who die in mine and mill and under rolling wheels; they make the slaughter possible by cheapening the estimate that is put on the value of a human life. Whosoever talks of "cheap" people, and of "lower" classes, and insists that some are especially valuable to God, and that others are their "inferiors," will go to hell, said Jesus; and I think He was right.

A little farther on in His life, we shall see how He proved it, and on what great natural fact He based His assertion. I have given you the exact meaning of the quoted passage, and the only meaning which may legitimately be drawn from it.

Turn now to the 12th chapter of Matthew and read the first eight verses.

The Sabbath . There you find that the disciples were crossing the fields on the Sabbath day, and that they plucked the ears of corn, and ate as they went. This gave great offense to the Pharisees. They were not offended because they took the grain, for, under the Jewish law, the right of the hungry wayfarer to life transcended the property rights of the owner of the field; none might say the famished man nay, if he chose to pluck and eat. It was not to a theft of grain that the Pharisees objected, but to the fact that the plucking and eating were done on the Sabbath day. The Pharisees believed that the one thing most valuable to God was their church with its institutions and observances. They would not break the Sabbath to feed a hungry man, or to heal a sick man, because they thought the Sabbath was more valuable to God than the man.

And so they complained to Jesus, and He answered them, "Have ye not heard what David did, when he was hungry; he and they that were with him?" and He went on to tell them from their own scriptures, in which, as I have said, He was letter-perfect, how David and his followers went into the temple and took the sacred shew bread and ate it - and God approved. "One standeth here," said Jesus, "greater than the temple."

"The (son of) man is lord of the Sabbath day." That is, God cares more for a hungry man than He does for a holy day or house. In the second chapter of Mark, where the same story is told, He adds, "The Sabbath was made for man, and not man for the Sabbath."

Organizations . Here is brought out and sharply defined the issue between Jesus and His opponents. They were exalting the temple, the worship, the Sabbath, the ceremonial; He exalted the man. They declared that God was working through humanity to build systems and institutions; He declared that God was working through systems and institutions to build humanity. And I, for one, agree with Jesus. I feel no reverence for buildings; even though they are magnificent structures, where the dim light falls through stained glass windows upon the sculptured forms of saints and angels, where robed priests chant in solemn cadence; these things move me little.

But when I stand in a schoolroom and look into the bright faces of a hundred, boys and girls - when I stand in the crowded marketplace, or in a mill or factory where my brothers and sisters toil to supply the needs of the world, and I remember that every soul before me contains possibilities as boundless as the universe itself; when I stand in the presence of this toiling, seeking, loving, suffering, glorious, common humanity, I bare my head and bow in reverence, for here, indeed, I am in the presence of Almighty God. One is here greater than the temple, greater than the Sabbath, greater than the system, greater than the institution, greater than the Church or State.

God has a higher call for man than the keeping of certain days and places holy. This whole earth is a holy place, because it is consecrated by the love of God to fulfill His purpose in unfolding the high destiny of man.

Little Children . In the 18th chapter of Matthew you will read how Jesus took a little child and set him in the midst, of them, and said; "Whosoever shall humble himself as this little child, the same shall be greatest in the kingdom of heaven"; and He went on to assert that whatsoever should offend the child had better be cast into the sea.

You will get a good idea of the prevailing misconception concerning Jesus and His times if you study the pictures you commonly see of the scene where He blessed the little children. He is always shown to us surrounded by prettily dressed women, who are bringing nice clean babies for Him to love and bless; and it looks very easy for one to humble himself as one of those.

But turn back to our description of the condition of the masses in His day, and you will get a different idea. That was a slave child that He set in the midst of them; unwashed, uncombed, covered with vermin and noisome sores repulsive to every sense; a child of the abyss, in the darkest period of the world's history.

And what could He mean by telling us to humble ourselves as such a child? Is it that we should be childlike in spirit, teachable, credulous? No; there is only one way. Stand beside that child of the gutter, and say; "Before God he is as good as I. He is entitled to everything that I claim for myself and for my children, and I will not rest until all that I demand for my own is his also." Then you will have humbled yourself as the little child by acknowledging his equality with you, and then you will begin to be great in the kingdom of heaven.

"W hosoever shall offend one of these little (slaves?) ones, it is better that a millstone shall be hanged about his neck, and he were cast into the sea." Yes, any man, or woman, or railroad system, or financial system, or industrial order or disorder that stands between the poor man's child and life, is under the curse of God. It is better that all the corn crops of a thousand years be lost, than that the least injustice shall be done to one such little child. That is what Jesus taught; and it is not to be wondered at that He was crucified.

Chapter 4 - His Teachings About Wealth

One day Jesus was teaching the people, and He said, in substance; "Why are you worried about things to eat, and to wear". Look at the birds; they have not a fraction of your intelligence; they do not know enough to sow, or reap, or gather provision for the future; and yet they have no famine. You, with your great intelligence, surely ought to be able to live with more ease and safety than the lower orders of life; yet the only fear and anxiety are to be found among men. Seek the kind of kingdom your Father wants; a perfectly righteous order of things, and you will have plenty of everything."

This is a rather free translation of Matthew 6:25-34, but it is a very accurate rendering of the meaning of the original; much more accurate than that given by the King James version.

And I wish here to give you a word of caution. I frequently receive letters from people who lay great stress on the interpretation of some particular passage from the New Testament, and even on that of some single word; as if the letter of it was a perfect and infallible guide. Now, remember that Jesus taught and spoke in the Aramaic, a dialect which had entirely supplanted the Hebrew among the Jews of Palestine, and that His sayings, in that language, were held in memory about seventy years before they appeared in the Greek, written in the manuscripts of the gospels; and that from the Greek they were translated into the English of 500 years ago, in our King James version. Five hundred years ago many words in our language carried meanings which are lost now; and so you will see how foolish it is to pin so much faith on single detached sayings and passages, which may not at all convey the meaning He gave to them. We never can understand him until we study his teachings as a connected whole.

Wealth for All . On the face of things it would look as if He told the truth when He said that there was no need for worry. There is no lack of the things needed, and where there is no lack there is no necessity for worry. This world would produce food, under intensive cultivation, for

more than ten times its present population. It would produce the fabrics wherewith to clothe ten times its present population finer than Solomon was arrayed in all his glory. It would furnish building material sufficient to erect a palace larger than the Capitol at Washington for every family now living, and there would be material enough left over to house another generation.

Our Father has provided the raw material for all the things essential to life, and He has provided a thousandfold more than we can use. The race, taken as a whole, is rich; immensely rich; it is only individuals within the race who are poor.

The satisfaction of human needs is a problem of machinery and organization, and the machinery is pretty well perfected; it is now, then, a matter of organization.

Seek the Father's Kingdom, says Jesus, and you solve the bread and butter problem. Does that sound like a rational interpretation of the passage we are speaking of? Turn to the 12th chapter of Luke, and read the parallel passage.

The Kingdom of God . Now, what did He mean by the kingdom of God? Practically all commentators agree, now, that He did not mean a distinct Heaven, which we cannot enter until we die; and they agree, also that He did not mean a church like the one we have now.

If you can conceive of the church as expanded until it filled the whole earth; all the people united in one, and all practicing what the churches preach now, that would be very like a Kingdom of God as Jesus describes it.

He illustrates it by showing that the birds know no anxiety; they live in the Father's kingdom. They all, alike, have access to the Supply. There is no bug trust, and no shrewd bird has, as yet, cornered the worm market. W hen, instead of going freely to the Great Supply, the birds begin to compete for the limited portions of it, there will begin to be an anxiety among them. There can be no Father's kingdom unless all can have equal access to the Great Supply.

Equality and Democracy. You will find this confirmed in the twenty-third chapter of Matthew, in the first twelve verses. Here He lays the foundation of the kingdom in the fact of the Fatherhood of God, and I will call the attention of the literalists especially to the fact that the sayings were addressed "to the multitude" as well as to His disciples.

He assures them all that God is their Father, and that they are brethren; and that hence, they should not compete for the best place at the feast. If, instead of struggling with each other, you will go lovingly to the feast together, is there not enough for all? Let there be no striving for mastery, or power over one another; just plain equality and democracy, says Jesus, and no one will have to bear a heavy burden anymore.

Suppose the father of a family should see his children gather around a table, where he had provided for them as bountifully as our Father has for us; and suppose that the largest boy should get to the table first and gather all the best food around his plate. W hen his little sister reaches for a nice piece of cake he slaps her; he strikes back the out stretched hands of the others, and says:

"Get away! Our father put this here, and I am the first one to get to it; so it is mine. Get away" (strike, push, shove) and, looking up to his parent, he addresses him thus: "Our father (biff), thy kingdom come (bang), thy will be done (whack)."

Would not that father say, "M y will will not be done until you, with your brothers and sisters, go together to the Supply I have provided."

And if the large boy should say then: "Well, father, I will hold it as your trustee, giving to the others as I think it best for them, and seeing that all is done decently and in order," would not the father say, "I do not want benevolence, or charity, or self-denial, or Sabbath observance, but that each one shall go freed to the Supply for all that he needs."

The idea of Jesus appears to be that if each one will go freely to the Supply, there can be no poverty or lack of any kind; and His idea appears to be sound. If the supply is super-abundant, and all go freely to it, how can anybody have lack? The trouble is that we have our eyes fixed, not on the Abundance, but on the Uppermost Place.

It is as if there were a mountain of gold, to which we might go for wealth, but on our way thither we find a few scattering nuggets which have been washed down by the rains, and we stop to fight for the possession of these fragments, and so lose the whole.

In this connection, look up the parallel passages in Luke, and note the one in the twenty-second chapter, where He cautions them against that most insidious of temptations, the desire to pose as a "benefactor." No benefactors are needed where all may go to the Supply. You are to serve by inviting men to the feast, not by handing them a few crumbs from your own plate. It is not possible that there should be benefactions, benefactors or charity in the kingdom of God; so long as there is need for these things we are not in His kingdom.

And how can we hope to establish the kingdom by practicing things which do not belong to it?

"Love Thy Neighbor"

It is in this light that we must consider His command to love one's neighbor as one's self. W hat does it mean, this loving one's neighbor as himself? Suppose my wife and I sit down to lunch; and there is nothing on the table but a crust of bread and a piece of pie. And suppose that I hastily grasp the pie, and say; "My dear, I certainly love you devotedly; I do wish you had some pie, also," and I swallow it, and leave her the crust; have I loved her as myself? If I love her as myself, I will desire pie for her as intensely as for myself, and I will try as hard to get it for her as for myself.

If I love you as myself, what I try to get for myself I will try to get for you, and what I try to get for my children I will try to get for your children, and I will no more rest under an injustice done to you or yours than if it had been done to me or mine.

And when we all desire for everybody all that we desire for ourselves, what is there for us to do but to stop competing for a part and turn to the abundance of the Great W hole, which is the Kingdom of God.

In the next chapter we will consider how the apostles went about solving the problems of supply, and why they failed.

Chapter 5 - The Apostles and Their Failure

No one who studies carefully the teachings of Jesus can doubt that by the phrases, "Kingdom of Heaven" and "Kingdom of God," He meant such a righteous adjustment of social relations as would have revolutionized the Society of His day; or which, if applied in our time, would revolutionize the society of this day.

You will get this idea pretty clearly if you study His use of the term "this world," and His comparison of the "world" with the kingdom. W hen He speaks of the "world" He never means the earth; He always refers to the existing social and governmental order; the world of men; organized society. He speaks of this world as a living, sentient thing; as loving, hating, etc.; and it can hardly be that He refers to the senseless clods and stones composing the material planet on which we live.

Thus in John 17:14, He says: "The world hath hated them, because they are not of the world."

In the same chapter He speaks of His disciples as being in the world, but not of the world; as being sent into the world; and He prays that the world may believe, and that the world may know. In the two preceding chapters He speaks of the world as being overcome. Follow this clue through all His teachings, and you must conclude that by the "world" He means the existing order of human relationships.

The World and the Kingdom . Having come to an understanding of this, we can appreciate the contrast He draws between the world and the Kingdom. His Kingdom, He says, is "not of this world"; that is, it is not on the same basis as the world's kingdoms. "If My kingdom were of this world, then would My servants fight" (John 18:36).

In the world's kingdoms they fight; in His Kingdom they co-operate.

In the world's kingdoms they sustain the relationship of master and servant; in His Kingdom, they are "friends" (John 15:15) (See also M atthew 23:10).

The world's kingdoms are divided against themselves (M atthew 12:25), but in God's Kingdom they do not try to conquer or master one another. That is the essential thought of the life of the Kingdom - that there shall be no seeking for power over other men; over against it He places the essential thought of the world-life, which is the strife for power, and for the uppermost place.

So, when they sought to make Him king by force (John 6:15), He refused, because that would have been placing His Kingdom on the world basis of strife and competition, and a kingdom over which Jesus ruled by force of arms would, after all, differ from the world kingdoms only in degree, and not in principle. The only kingdom in the establishment of which He could assist was the Father's Kingdom; a co-operative commonwealth, in which all should have access on equal terms to God, and to the Great Supply.

So He sends His followers out, not to fight or conquer, but to go as lambs among wolves, and by teaching and living to transform the insane and struggling world into a vast brotherhood. He believed that He had overcome the world by His demonstration, and that it must soon come to its end.

The End of the World . This brings up another point for our consideration. W hen He speaks of the "end of the world" it is apparent that He is not referring to some tremendous cataclysm which shall destroy the planet, but to a social change; a world revolution. In the twenty-fourth chapter of Matthew, He does, indeed, give some symbolical pictures of the darkness of the sun and moon, etc., which He quotes from the prophecies; but as we shall see in a future chapter, the "coming of the son of man" meant to Him, not His own personal return to establish a spiritual force-kingdom, but the awakening of racial M an, and his entrance into his heritage. W hen M an awakes and enters into his own, the world will be ended and the Kingdom will begin; that is the Coming of Man, which the prophets foretold.

That is the way Jesus interpreted them, as you will see if you study Him carefully and without prejudice. He does not appear to have had any idea that the planet would "come to an end"; or that He would actually come in personal presence to do what He steadfastly refused to do while here - set up a kingdom based on force.

The apostles caught this concept of the Kingdom, and they set forth with joyous confidence to build a united and harmonious world.

Read the second and fourth chapters of the Acts, and read the writings of the early Christian fathers, and you will see that their idea was not to build an institution for worship, in a bad world, but to build the world itself into a righteous, united and orderly society. Property was held in common, and there was no poverty among them which was not shared by all, and no riches which were not enjoyed by all.

The early Christian societies were little commonwealths, and the inspiring purpose to which they held with intense enthusiasm was the building of the world into one great commonwealth.

The apostles were communist organizers, and the purpose of Jesus as understood by them was the establishment of a communistic state which should grow up within the kingdoms of the World, and absorb them all, not by force, but by conquest of truth; by evangelizing the world, by educating it to the brotherhood ideals and methods.

Their dream was a world of Man, where the united efforts of all should center in the development of the little child; it was this glorious vision which gave virility and power to their preaching, and it was the loss of this vision which cost the church its spiritual power. The church of today is alive in proportion as it receives this world-vision; as it sees the kingdom and helps reorganize society.

W hy Communism Fails . We may here consider for a moment why the communistic experiment failed, and we shall find the reason easy to get at. Communism has always failed, and always will fail, because it interferes with the Great Purpose, which is the complete development of the individual soul. It extinguishes the individual in the mass, and takes all initiative from him. Seeking to prevent him from gaining power over other men, it robs him of power over himself. It destroys individuality for man can develop only by the free proprietary use of everything he is individually capable of using.

Capitalism robs the majority of men of the opportunity to make proprietary use of the things necessary for their individual development; Communism would rob all men of this opportunity. In this, both are the opposites of Christian socialism.

Christian Socialism . Socialism would tremendously extend private property. Its cardinal doctrine is that the individual should own, absolutely and without question, everything which they need or can use individually; and that the right to hold private property should be limited only when we come to those things which a man cannot operate without exploiting other men. Man, under socialism, may acquire and hold all that he can use for his own development; but he may not own that which makes him master of another man.

As we approach socialism, the millions of families who are now propertyless will acquire and own beautiful homes, with the gardens and the land upon which to raise their food; they will own horses and carriages, automobiles and pleasure yachts; their houses will contain libraries, musical instruments, paintings and statuary, all that a person may need for the soul-growth of themselves and theirs, they shall own and use as they will.

But highways, railroads, natural resources, and the great machines will be owned and operated by organized society, so that all who will may purchase the product upon equal terms. Socialism, when properly understood, offers us the most complete individualism, while communism would submerge the individual in the mass.

The apostles failed because communism is a failure in the nature of things, while the world, at that time, had not evolved far enough to make socialism possible. They tried to establish for all a life which was only possible to a few.

Chapter 6 - The Source of Power

Jesus ascribed all His marvelous power to the mental relationship which existed between Himself and the Father. He uses the terms Father and God interchangeable, and says: "My father, of whom ye say that he is your God" (John 8:54).

And in His talk with the Samaritan woman, He explains clearly His conception of God, declaring that "God is Spirit" (Not A Spirit, as the King James version has it), and that He is not to be worshipped in some particular place like Jerusalem, or on some specially consecrated mountain, but may be approached, or worshipped in spirit and in truth, anywhere.

The Father, as described by Jesus, is Universal Spirit, working in all, through all, and FOR ALL. He describes this spirit as making the sun to shine, and causing the rain to fall, and so as being the POW ER behind nature; as clothing the lilies of the field, and causing the hair to grow on man's heads, and so as being the one and only LIFE; as quickening and leading men to truth and so as being the one and only INTELLIGENCE.

Every man is a God, according to Jesus, because it is Spirit which lives in man; He said to them: "Ye are Gods" (John 10:34). Spirit holds the earth in its orbit, makes the sun rise, sends the rain, and causes the coming of seedtime and harvest; Spirit lives in the lily and clothes it finer than Solomon was arrayed in all his glory; Spirit lives in man.

There is only one power, only one life, only one intelligence.

Unity of Man in God . As I have said, Jesus ascribed all His power to His conscious unity of mind with this One Intelligence. "I and my father are one," said He. "I do always his will."

And He went on to declare that because He always did the will of Spirit, Universal Spirit worked in and through Him. "I do always

those things that please him," said he (John 8:29). "I come, not to do mine own will, but the will of him that sent me." "I seek not mine own will, but the will of him" - and so on.

He made it perfectly plain that it was because of this unity of mind with the Father - which we call cosmic consciousness - that the Father could work through Him.

Because I will to do his will, said Jesus, my father and I act as one; and so it is not I that do the works, but the Father that worketh in me. He was consciously one with the one Spirit, and so all power in heaven and earth was at His service; He was consciously one with the one Life, and so He could transfigure His body, and heal others; "there went out from him a virtue (a realization of truth) that healed them all"; He was consciously one with the one Intelligence, and so all knowledge and all wisdom were His.

This is a point we must not lose sight of; that all that there is in the life of Jesus which transcends the ordinary, He positively declares to be due to His cosmic consciousness; to unity of mind and will with the All-Spirit.

Cosmic Consciousness . I will quote you a few more passages on this point; "He that sent me is true, whom ye know not; but I know him" (John 7:28-29). "I know him, and keep his saying" (John 8:55). "The son can do nothing of himself, but what he seeth the father do" (John 5:19). "As the father knoweth me, even so know I the father" (John 10:15). To "know" the father can have but one meaning; and that is to be conscious of Spirit; to have my own consciousness so unified with the consciousness of Spirit that what Spirit knows I know; what Spirit sees I see; and what Spirit does, I do.

My father is greater than I; I proceeded forth and came from Him; but if I unite with Him in consciousness, He is in me and I in Him, and He and I are one.

Jesus declares that this cosmic consciousness is the source of all power; He demonstrates that it is perfect health, both in His own person, and by healing others; "and this is life eternal to KNOW thee" (John 17:3). He asserts that it gives perfect wisdom - "The father loveth the son, and showeth him all things." "My judgment is true; for I am not alone, but I and the father" (John 8:16).

And He asserts that it is wealth; "All things that the father hath are mine" (John 16:15).

Christ's Brothers . He does not trace His power to something peculiar about His birth, but to His conscious unity with Spirit.

He does not say that God is His father alone, but that He is our father. He says; "One is your father, and all ye are brethren."

He says in the sermon on the mount; "It is your father who feeds and cares for you; be his children in mind and will, as you are in fact."

He does not assert that He is a demi-god, and that we are men; but that He is God, and we may be God, too, if we will; "He that willeth to do the will of God, shall know"; "shall enter the kingdom," and so on.

"The works that I do, ye shall do also; and greater works than these shall ye do."

The consciousness that He had, He seems to think quite possible for all of us; "That they may all be one," he prays, in the seventeenth chapter of John, "as thou, Father, art in me, and I in thee, that they may be one in us." "I in them, and thou in me, that they may be made perfect in one." What He is, we can any or all of us become, He says.

Jesus' Relationship to God . It is not within the scope of this little book to study whether Jesus really was born in a different way from other people; that inquiry must be reserved for a more pretentious work. But this is quite certain, that He Himself made no claim to being different from the rest of us, except as to the extent of His consciousness.

He was conscious of a relationship with Spirit which the world knew nothing about; this relationship existed for the world as well as for Himself, whenever the world would recognize it, and enter into it. And for all to enter into this conscious unity with Spirit would save the world from sin, sickness, ignorance and poverty; it would establish the Kingdom of God.

He could pray for no greater good than that they might be "one with the Father," even as He was one with the Father. To be one with the Father is to be one with Spirit; and to be one with Spirit is to so harmonize with it that thought, life, power, and wisdom shall come in a continuous inflow from Spirit into our minds and bodies.

M an's Relationship to God . There is, according to Jesus, one Spirit who is all the power there is, all the life there is, and all the intelligence there is; and this Spirit has children, who are of the same substances as Himself, and who have power to think independently, and to separate themselves in consciousness from Him.

And the power to think independently implies the possibility of thinking erroneously; if man separates himself in consciousness from God, he is sure to fall into error, for he can see only an infinitesimal portion of the truth.

Man's life, man's power, and man's wisdom decrease in exact proportion to the extent of his separation in consciousness from God.

Jesus found a world of men who had lost the consciousness of God, and because of doing so had become afflicted with the most horrible diseases; had fallen into the vilest depths of sin and debauchery; had sunk to the lowest levels of poverty and misery, and were in danger of losing life itself. To this lost and struggling world, He gave a demonstration of the possibilities of a life of cosmic consciousness - of conscious unity with Spirit. He demonstrated power over nature by calming the storm, and precipitating the food elements from the atmosphere to feed the hungry multitude; He demonstrated the power of Life to heal the sick; He demonstrated the W isdom which is beyond the limited consciousness of Man, and He demonstrated wealth; and finally, He demonstrated power over death.

And He told them how He did what He did, and how any other man might do the same, and even greater works.

The method of attaining cosmic consciousness we will consider in the next chapter.

Chapter 7 - Attaining Cosmic Consciousness

"And this is Life Eternal: to know God."

Cosmic consciousness or conscious unity with Eternal Spirit can only be attained by a continuous and sustained effort on the part of man. The extension of consciousness always requires a mental effort; and this mental effort, when it is a seeking for unity with Spirit, constitutes prayer.

Prayer is an effort of the human mind to become acquainted with God. It is not an effort to establish a relationship which does not exist, but to fully comprehend and recognize a relationship which already exists. Prayer can have but one object, and that is unity with Spirit; for all other things are included in that.

We do not really seek, through prayer, to get health, peace, power or wealth; we seek to get unity with God; and when we get unity with God, health, peace, power and wealth are ours without asking. Study the intercessory prayer, as it is called, in the seventeenth chapter of John, and you will see that Jesus asks nothing for men except that they may be one in mind with God. This is the one thing needful; all other things are contained in it.

Whoever has full spiritual consciousness has health, peace, power and wealth.

Oneness Through Prayer and Will. Jesus laid great stress on prayer in His teachings, and demonstrated His reliance upon it in His daily practice. The gospels abound with references to His praying; to His going apart to pray, continuing all night in prayer, and so on.

It is evident that His consciousness that He and the Father were one was only retained by persistently and continuously affirming and reaffirming the fact. This fact, it must be remembered, is in direct contradiction to our objective consciousness.

We appear to think, live, move and have our being entirely in ourselves and of ourselves; our physical senses deny the existence of a God. God is not found by extending the outward or objective consciousness. "God is Spirit," said Jesus, "and they who approach Him must approach Him through their own spirits."

To attain cosmic consciousness, the effort of prayer must be, first to arouse to activity the spirit in man and second, to unite that spirit in conscious union with God.

The spirit of man - the ego - the man himself, is aroused whenever the will acts.

Only the man himself can will; and when he wills it is his whole personality which comes into action.

We see, then, that Jesus was perfectly scientific in laying down His first requirement for attaining cosmic consciousness - that one must will to do the will of God.

He plainly ascribes His own power to His setting His will to do the will of Cosmic Spirit; and He says;

"He that willeth to do the will of God shall know."

To will to do the will of the Father, to keep His sayings, to do His works; this was the first step toward unity. And the next was the prayer of faith.

The Prayer of Faith. The prayer of faith is clearly described in Mark 11:23-24. "Whosoever shall say unto this mountain, Be thou removed, and be thou cast into the sea; and shall not doubt in his heart, but shall believe that those things which he saith shall come to pass; he shall have whatsoever he saith.

"Therefore, I say unto you, what things soever ye desire when ye pray, believe that ye receive them (now), and ye shall have them."

We see, here, that the prayer of faith cannot be offered twice for the same thing. As soon as you have asked, if you have real faith, your prayer changes to an affirmation of possession. Having willed to do the will of God, and having asked God to receive you into Himself, nothing is left you but to declare, "I and my Father are one."

This is the point which has been missed by most commentators - that the prayer of faith, when uttered, becomes an affirmation of possession. You cannot continue to pray for a thing when you believe that you receive it; you can only return thanks and assert that it is yours.

The Process of Receiving . First, will to do the will of God, and then (2) pray that you may be one with Him; and then (3) affirm, "I and my father are one."

And when you have definitely established in your consciousness the fact of your unity with Spirit, then draw your deductions of health, peace, power and wealth from this fact, and affirm them; otherwise you may not demonstrate them, for while they are all included in the fact of your unity with God, the mere assertion of that may not bring all the corollaries to your consciousness.

W hen the disciples came to Jesus asking Him to teach them to pray, He gave them the Lord's prayer; and it begins; "Thy kingdom come." When one has said that, he has asked for all there is; in the Kingdom of God no one would be without daily bread, or suffer evil; but these things are included in the prayer in order to make the thing prayed for more definite to the understanding.

So, the general affirmation of unity with God is not sufficiently definite to bring us health, peace, power and wealth; we do not clearly understand that these are included, and it is better to affirm them. But we must be definite and specific in our understanding of the fact of our unity with God.

"That Mind which was in Christ Jesus" . "I and my Father are one." That is good, but it does not convey the idea to the modern mind with sufficient distinctness.

"There is one Intelligence, and I am one with that Intelligence." Better, but somewhat clumsy.

"There is one MIND, and I am that MIND." That is a most clear-cut and concise statement of the fact; it would be hard to put it more tersely.

"There is ONE MIND." W hen you say that, think of the one Intelligence, permeating all things, vitalizing all things, giving coherence and purpose to all things. Get your thought fixed on this MIND, so that it seems to you that you can see and feel it! Then say: "I AM that MIND."

It is that MIND which is speaking, when I speak; which is acting when I act.

I-AM-that-MIND.

It takes affirming and reaffirming to get this fact fixed in consciousness, but all the time you put into the work is most profitably spent. You can well afford to go, as Jesus did, into the desert to fast and meditate for forty days; you can well afford to spend whole nights in prayer, if by doing so you can arrive at a full consciousness of your unity with God.

For then you will have entered the Kingdom.

"There is one MIND, and I am that MIND." Say it continuously, and always when you say it, try to comprehend all that it means. You; you who speak, are eternal mind; eternal power; eternal life.

All things are yours, and all things are possible unto you, when once you have banished the false idea of separateness from your consciousness.

Your word will be with power, and you will speak as one having authority; you will demonstrate health, power, wealth and wisdom,

when the consciousness that you are the ETERNAL ONE has obtained complete possession of your mind, objective and subjective.

And you can bring this about; only faith and continuing in affirmation while you will to do the will of God, are required.

Chapter 8 - Demonstration and Attainment

After you have affirmed and reaffirmed your unity with the One Mind until that unity has become a fact present to your consciousness, the next step is to become Life-conscious.

Understand that the Mind is a living mind; that it is life, itself. If you are Mind, you are also Life. There is only one Life, which is in all, and through all; and you are that Life.

So, follow your first affirmation with this; "That MIND is eternal, and it is LIFE; I am that MIND, and I am ETERNAL LIFE."

Repeat this until you have thoroughly stamped it upon your mentality, both conscious and subconscious; until you habitually think of yourself as life, and as eternal life. Now, you habitually think of yourself as a dying being, or as one moving on toward age and decay; this is an error, born of holding separate consciousness. Meet every suggestion of age, decay or death with the positive assertion: "I am ETERNAL LIFE."

Jesus said: "And this is life eternal; to know thee, the LIVING God." To know God is to be conscious of your unity with Him; howelse can you know him?"

Health Consciousness . After Life-consciousness is attained, the step to Health- consciousness is easy. The One Mind is the living stuff from which you are made; and it is Pure Life. Life must be Health; it is inconceivable that an inflow of pure life should carry with it anything but health. A fountain cannot send forth sweet and bitter at the same time. A good tree cannot bring forth corrupt fruit. Light hath no fellowship with darkness. The One Mind cannot know disease; can have no consciousness of disease.

The consciousness of disease is an error, the result of judging by appearances; and we judge by appearances only so long as we retain the separate consciousness. One cannot be Life-conscious and conscious of disease at the same time; when we become fully life- conscious we lose the disease-consciousness.

So, the next affirmation is; "That Mind knows no disease; I am that Mind and I am HEALTH." Affirm it with faith; it will cure every sickness, if the affirmation is made in the consciousness that you and your Father are one.

Power Consciousness . Next comes power-consciousness; and the affirmation for this is: "That Mind is the source of all POW ER, and cannot know doubt nor fear; I am that Mind, and I am PEACE and POW ER."

It needs no argument to show that the source of all power cannot be afraid of anything; what could there be for it to be afraid of? Nor can the source of all power have doubts as to its being able to do any conceivable thing, or to cope with any possible combination of circumstances; what is there that all the power there is cannot do?

It is only when you conceive of yourself as separate from this power that you begin to have doubts as to your ability to do things; it is only as you hold this separate consciousness that you can be afraid.

Jesus never showed any doubt; nor did He ever manifest fear. He knew that no harm could come to Him, against His will; and none did. He was not crucified because His enemies gained a victory over Him; He went voluntarily to the cross, to make a demonstration which should finally show the truth to His disciples. "No man takes my life," said He, "I lay it down of myself; I have power to lay it down, and I have power to take it again" (John 10:18).

To have power-consciousness gives poise; poise is the peaceful consciousness of power and is the result of affirming unity with power until it becomes a present fact in consciousness. "Peace I leave with you; my peace I give unto you. Let not your heart be troubled; neither let it be afraid."

You cannot keep your heart from being afraid if you retain consciousness of yourself as something apart from Power. So, understand and affirm that you are one with Power.

W isdom Consciousness . Wisdom-consciousness is next. Power without wisdom may be a dreadful and destructive thing, like the strength of the runaway horse; and power can be constructive only when wisely applied. So we must affirm the fact of our wisdom. The One Mind, being the source of all things, must know all things from the beginning; must know all truth.

The mind which knows all truth cannot be mistaken; mistakes are caused by a partial knowledge of the truth. Such a mind cannot knowerror.

Knowing ALL truth, it can only act along the lines of perfect truth; it can only entertain in consciousness the idea of perfect truth.

It cannot know good from evil; it can know only the good. To recognize anything as evil, a mind must have only a partial knowledge, and a limited consciousness. W hat seems to be evil is always the result of partial knowledge. W here knowledge is perfect, there is no evil; and no one can be conscious of that which does riot exist.

"God is light and in him is no darkness at all." "God is of too pure eyes to behold evil, and cannot look upon eniquity."

When we become conscious of ALL truth, we lose the consciousness of evil.

W ith complete consciousness judgment becomes impossible, for there is nothing to judge. You do not have to exercise judgment when you know the right way; you do not sit in judgment on others where there is no evil.

So Jesus said; "Ye judge after the flesh; I judge no man." "I am come, not to judge the world, but to save the world." "The Father judgeth no man."

W here evil and error are non-existent, there can be no judgment. To rise above the error of belief in evil, use this affirmation; "That Mind knows only TRUTH, and knows ALL truth; I am that Mind, and I am KNOWLEDGE and WISDOM ."

Wealth Consciousness . Having attained consciousness of eternal life, of health, power, and wisdom, what else do you need? Wealth-consciousness; the assurance of affluence and abundance.

The one Mind is the original substance, from which all things proceed forth. There is only one element; all things are formed of one stuff.

Science is now precipitating sugar, coloring matter, and other substances from the atmosphere; that seems to be akin to what Jesus did when He fed the multitude, in the so-called miracles of the loaves and fishes. The elements which compose all visible nature are in the atmosphere, waiting to be organized into form; and the atmosphere itself is only a condensed and palpable form of the one original substance - Spirit - God.

All things are made from, and made of, one living intelligent substance; One Mind, and you are that Mind. Therefore, you are the substance from which all things are made, and you are also the Power which makes and forms; you are wealth and abundance, for you are all there is.

So, affirm; "All things, created and uncreated, are in that Mind; I am that Mind, and I am WEALTH and PLENTY."

I Am the Way, Truth, Life . Lastly, say; "I am the WAY, and the TRUTH, and the LIFE; the LIGHT in me shines out to bless the world."

This will give you love-consciousness: the will to bless, and the will to love. Eternal life; health; power and peace; wisdom; wealth; and love; when you are conscious of all these, you have attained cosmic consciousness; you are in Christ and Christ is in you.

Statement of Being.

There is one Mind, and I AM that Mind.

That Mind is eternal, and it is Life.

I am that Mind, and I am ETERNAL LIFE.

That Mind knows no disease; I am that Mind, and I am HEALTH.

That Mind is the source of all Power, and cannot know doubt nor fear; I am that Mind, and I am POWER and PEACE.

That Mind knows only Truth and knows ALL truth; I am that Mind, and I am KNOW LEDGE and WISDOM .

All things created and uncreated, are in that Mind; I am that Mind, and I am WEALTH and PLENTY.

I am the WAY, and the TRUTH, and the LIFE; the LIGHT in me shines out to bless the world.

Made in the USA
Coppell, TX
05 April 2023

15264664R00020